Ensemble

Poems by Linda M. Lewis

Kansas City   Spartan Press   Missouri

Spartan Press
Kansas City, MO
spartanpresskc@gmail.com

Copyright © Linda M. Lewis, 2019
First Edition 1 3 5 7 9 10 8 6 4 2
ISBN: 978-1-950380-35-0
LCCN: 2019942448

Design, edits and layout: Jason Ryberg
Cover image: Debbie Wagner
Title page image: Jim Turner
Author photo: Jim Turner
All rights reserved. No part of this publication may be reproduced or transmitted in any form or by any means, electronic or mechanical, including photocopying, recording or by info retrieval system, without prior written permission from the author.

Acknowledgments:

An earlier version of "After Tasting" was published in *Plainsongs* and "Delayed Flight" in the online journal *59 Review*; "Lillian's Version," "Snakebite," and "Temperance Warrior" appeared in the premier issue of *Konza Poetry Poetry Project*.

My sincere gratitude to Spartan Press and Editor Jason Ryberg. Additional gratitude to painter Debbie Wagner for permission to reproduce her "Thinking Through" on the cover. Thanks to Jim Turner for permitting the use of his photograph on the inside title page.

A hearty thank you to the insightful critics in my writing circle: Lori Brack, Majkin Holmquist, Aubrey Streit Krug, Greg LeGault, and Kristin Van Tassel. Thanks to Patricia Traxler for her encouragement. Also to Myrne Roe, Jackie Ash, Sharon Texley, and Amanda Marbais—my previous writing group, now scattered.

An extra big dose of love to my supportive family: Terry and Tom Hall, Trudy Lewis, Michael Barrett, and grandchildren Sylvia, Eddie, Madeline, Cliff, Jude, Lauren, and Nick. Special appreciation to my love, Frank Lewis, who found his way into my life and into several of these poems.

CONTENTS

Bearing Witness / 1

Delayed Flight / 2

Trapeze Act / 4

Stalking Baryshnikov / 5

Burning in Her Bones / 6

Lillian's Version / 7

Aretha's Last Encore / 8

Final Curtain / 9

The King's Concubine / 10

Defiance Writ Large / 11

Trojan Princess Dead at Argos / 12

Sunday Morning Charity / 13

Sacrament / 14

Mother Teresa's Tautology / 15

After Tasting / 16

Snakebite / 17

In My Garden / 18

Looking Back / 19

Ravenous / 20

Prelude / 21

Suppliant / 22

Reaper / 23

Child-keeping / 24

Concord Mothers / 25

Ocean Camping / 26

Framing the Scene / 27

The Brontës Sit for a Portrait / 28

Photogenic / 29

iconic dress / 30

Stitchery / 31

Selfhood / 32

Sophia Andreevna Dreams of Trees / 33

Anne's Soliloquy / 35

Driving West from Mena, Arkansas / 37

Obsession / 39

A Litany / 41

Frida Imagines / 42

Woman Wall, 2019 / 43

Tables Turned / 44

Penelope's Lament / 45

Love Letter / 46

Only Mother milked the cow / 48

Temperance Warrior / 49

For Peace, Bread and Roses / 51

Early Redbud / 52

Just Ourselves and Immortality / 53

Modern Pastoral / 54

Notes / 55

Not Spring is unreal to me,

I have the tree-flowers by heart.

Love, twenty years, forty years, my life

is unreal to me.

- Denise Levertov

Bearing Witness

Just we three share the pier at twilight,
you casting and casting some tempting
lure into the bay, I wrapped in my sweater,
lolling on wooden planks still warm from
midday sun drench. A Great Blue Heron
perches on a pier rail, observes your
   throw-pause-reel rhythm,
      awaits an outcome.

The creature's neck shapes an elegant S.
Sword-sharp feathers, like matching hatpins,
pierce the crown of her black velvet chapeau.
Her bodice plumage resembles willow leaves,
   silver-dipped, stitched to a gown
      fit for a soirée.

Darkness palms shore, sea, sky. You reel in
your line. We witness this transformation:
she stretches, flexes, lifts off—a vision
above the bay, against the dark, wings
   white as angel raiment flounced
      in cerulean blue.

Delayed Flight

Alerted by a cacophony
of low-soaring shrieks,
I gaze upward to an
ascent of geese that barely
clears the catalpa tree.
But this is Memorial Day—
city asleep in morning calm,
campus emptied; my seniors
degreed, departed, flown.
Weeks ago Canada geese
staged the annual flyover;
their checkmark slashed
the papery skies of March.
How to account for this late
departure announced in
such clamor. Are these the
dying generation wearied by
seasons carried on the wing?
Perhaps the hip who cruised
Gulf hangouts as their elders
lifted off? The laggards must
have watered last night on
Smoky River. They risk today a
sixty-percent chance of rain,
hail, cloud-shredding thunder.

They pull up sharp, dwindle in
my line of sight. I whisper them
Godspeed, charge them to
level off in a current that lifts
them weightless in flight.

Trapeze Act

If falling were performance art, I would have been a star.
As a girl I fell off a horse, a sycamore branch, my green
Schwinn bike, the monkey bars. Fell (as scars attest)
onto gravel, broken glass, barbed wire fence.

Later I fell for a pick-up line, a pair of mellifluent brown eyes,
a sob story, compliment, guarantee and gimmick. I fell
in love. For love. To love. With love. Love of every
tint and shade. And every preposition.

At the circus a daring girl costumed in spangles casts off the fly
bar and into a brilliant black void that fills the bigtop. She
sails like a dragonfly, freefalls into the fists of a muscled
catcher who saves, lifts, enfolds her.

I had aspired to be a flyer—graceful, dazzling, death-defying.
But my talent is off-timing, missteps, the graceless fall. In
the last act, final scene, I stand fixed in place,
raised arms outstretched to receive you.

Stalking Baryshnikov

At the Orpheum stage door
after his bare-torso Corsaire
had spun and leaped and soared—
a body sculpting motion and
movement singing passion—
we waited for our golden-haired
god of dance to emerge into muted
glow of the theater exit, blow kisses,
glissade into the back seat of a
limousine, vanish in traffic of an
ink-black city night, leaving a score
of stranded Eurydices stunned by
a glimpse of Misha's magic.

Burning in Her Bones

Between Pentecost and the Rapture
Sister Aimee cruised into Sin City
with only a Bible and a tambourine.

At Angelus Temple Aimee performed
vaudeville sermons on a stage set—
spotlight haloing her bottle-blonde
marcel, her body shimmering in
angelwingwhite crêpe de chine.

Sister preached the Gospel of Showbiz:
That Jesus will soon descend dancing
bare white feet on dry-ice clouds,
Godlight sparking off his lambwhite
raiment, Hollywood-handsome face.

Lillian's Version

That prissy little Quaker trick-shooter was done for. There, I said it and reckoned it so until Bill Cody concocted a quarrel, knowing I would up and quit his Wild West shebang, leave the door open for Little Miss Sure Shot and her fawning Frank Butler to waltz right back under the big top. That girl sure didn't cotton to sharing a spotlight. Had a jealous streak wider than the Mighty Mo. When I showed up, way younger than Buffalo Bill's female firing wonder, she scissored years off herself quicker than you can pluck ticks from a dog's hide. She seen that Queen Victoria took a shine to Lillian Smith instead of Annie Oakley, and that rubbed her raw as a new-laid egg in a Ohio farmyard. Such a show-off: blam-blam-blamming clay pigeons like champagne corks popping, blasting ashes off the Kaiser's cigar. But her shotgun never shattered glass balls like my Winchester. Show folks can't keep a lid on, so I heard of her disdain over my flirty ways and fancy duds, her disgust at my grammar. But I seen it didn't bother Her Highness Queen Victoria none. My sharpshooting days are over. My lowdown German artist run off and left me like my barkeeper, lawman and bronc buster. None of them a stayer like Annie's Frank. I'll give her that. They say he starved himself after she died. I'm alone in Bliss, Oklahoma. Just me and my dogs and rifles and some tarnished trophies. In Bliss.
I wonder where Annie Oakley is.

Aretha's Last Encore

Today they buried the diva
of Detroit. For the gala she
wore a sparkly gold gown and
sequin-heeled stilettos—
perfectly matched to her
24-carat gold-plated coffin
lined with champagne velvet.
It was her fourth regal costume
change while lying in state—
from frothy crimson lace to
rose gold knit to a shimmering
frock of powder blue. The
funeral was an eight-hour
extravaganza with a cast
of celebrities performing their
respect. Singing, clapping,
praising, shouting rocked
Greater Grace Temple to its
rooftop. A cortege of 120 pink
Cadillacs and a white vintage
hearse. Pastel roses—enormous
mounds of them. Today the
Queen of Soul staged her exit
in a pageant beseeming royalty.

Final Curtain

The Queen adores Parisian silks and farthingales,
France's rhymes and roundels, its southern vintage
and rich cuisine. Her style earns English disdain
from a cooler, plainer, less exotic race—common
folk with no palate for *paté de fois gras*, no ear
for phonemes that buzz and vibrate in the brain.
Triumphant in act two, black-eyed Anne Boleyn
turns out the Spanish consort, earns encores in
the royal bed, bears a daughter but no son. What
terror in coitus: the corpulent King, flailing and
sweating to plant his seed and save a dynasty,
lowers his royal tun onto her little belly. What
fury over dead heirs interred in the womb of
that Gallic witch who seduced him to adultery.
A thousand days from the jubilant fête when
the blithe young Queen in purple velvet glided
up the Thames for crowning, dawns the May
morning when a skilled swordsman from Calais
will sever her slender neck. Drama demands its
due of hopeful lust and bloated rage; in the
wings the French swordsman awaits his cue.

The King's Concubine

She was by no means the first wife to conceive
while her soldier was gone to war. Yet the
story of comely Bathsheba, a name for promise,
was beyond ordinary deceit. King David, former
Bethlehem shepherd, poet and psalm-singer,
watched her bathe in a villa across the way.
Bathsheba the delectable, her skin the tint of rare
parchment, hair black as ravens' feathers, body as
tunable as any lyre David had ever stroked. The
royal voyeur acquired Uriah's wife in royal style;
he came, saw, and conquered—though possibly not
in that order. To secure his mistress, the king
choreographed Uriah's death in battle. Even
instructed his general to place the props and direct
the scene. After her requisite days of mourning,
Bathsheba was lodged at the palace, without
consent of Michal, King David's royal queen.

Defiance Writ Large

Beside great Caesar, I ruled the earth,
dispatched armies to march, slaves to
fetch figs and dates, women to braid
and coil my onyx tresses.

My golden barge with silver oars plied
the Nile; beneath perfumed sails in
regal cloth-of-gold, I rivaled the
Roman Venus and Egypt's Isis.

Valiant Antony I entranced with
Alexandria's largesse, succulent feast
and wine of sweetest vintage—the
wealth of pharaohs' palace.

A lesser Caesar now holds Egypt's queen
a prisoner, threatens torture, would have
me pelted with insults and garbage
from filthy plebeian masses.

Escape arrives in a contraband vessel of
figs. Venom will flow like the Nile through
rivers of my body. I will show them
what death befits a goddess.

Trojan Princess Dead at Argos

Because Apollo's priestess declined to get it on
with a god, she was knocked up with Truth.
Accustomed as he was to taking mortal women
for his pleasure, said immortal with a kiss spat
into Cassandra's mouth a double-edged gift,
excused his rape on grounds that the votary
was a teasing bitch, she had it coming, she
wanted it. Otherwise why the gauzy peplos
that slipped off her shoulder as she pored
over parchment scrolls in Apollo's temple?
Anyway, there was her uppity penchant
for learning (while normal girls flirted in the
agora with breast-plated warriors of Ilium).
When she foresaw that Paris—besotted
by a whore—would torch the homeland,
when she shredded Helen's golden veil,
prudent father Priam locked her up
in a dungeon, safest place for a wild-eyed,
disheveled prophetess whose ravings
always gave the Greeks an edge. She saw
armed Achaeans crouched inside the belly
of a wooden horse, heard the tremor of their
weapons echo in the dark, her own cry as Ajax
dragged her from Athena's refuge to ravish
and sell her to the Greek commander. In a
vision, she staunched Agamemnon's blood,
was blinded by glints off the two-edged blade
that violated her. But she proved this axiom:
beware of sorry-ass gods bearing gifts.

Sunday Morning Charity

Beneath shadowed mountains stacked above
lapping Adriatic waves stretches red-roofed
Kotor, a city whose medieval walls snake
drunkenly among pinnacles of Montenegro.
Brick-paved mazes of alleys and streets converge
at St. Tryphon Cathedral, where a feline
congregation claims the sun-streaked piazza.
Brindled cats, spotted cats, tabby cats,
sleek-skinny cats—promiscuous, prolific—
take their leisure. They stretch, preen, tumble,
pounce; they nibble fish fragments and crusty
bread scraps tithed by Saturday-night cafés.
Heathen Kotor cats ignore tourists crowding
fragrant coffee shops, a cassocked priest
sprinting up church steps, early drinkers
who swipe beer foam from whisker stubble
and lap up a Sunday hour at Scala Santa.
One thin-limbed pregnant Romany—wilting
skirt, bludgeoned shoes, tangled mane—
begs alms too beneath St. Tryphon's tower.

Sacrament

Sidling around the crowd in the Pharisee's house,
she approaches the rabbi as if invited. We know
this Magdalene, have seen her with Galileans,
seated among the faithful—those kohl-lined eyes
that follow him, unseemly, adoring. She plants
her smallish person and he pauses mid-sentence,
too late now for Peter or another to escort her
discreetly from the place. Did we leave boats and
nets to see his mission hindered by this whore?
Kneeling before him, she breaks open a jar of
spikenard. The fragrance floats. She removes his
sandals, cups by turn each heel in her scented palm,
baptizes both feet in valerian oil. Then casts aside
her veil, loosens blue-black waves that cascade down
her spine, ripple about her radiant face. She makes
obeisance as she weeps; her hands spread the flowing
mass that spills over, across, around his yielding feet.

Mother Teresa's Tautology

(from her meditations)

Deep is the conflict
within my soul.
I smile at the world;
my face a mask, a cloak.
Even deep as thoughts can
reach, all is darkness.
I must cherish darkness
because Jesus prayed
in dark Gethsemane.
To possess God, I must
allow Him to possess me.
But I became the bride
of Christ and my beloved
divorced me. I have
forsaken all for God yet
God has forsaken me.
When I call on Him,
I hear only silence.
When I look to heaven,
I see a barren mirage.
My doubts are daggers
that pierce my soul.
  O God—
if there be a God—
forgive my unbelief.

After Tasting

You, Apple Girl, in mutiny unsealed an enigma,
    Released a cohort of vices trapped inside.
    Did ambrosial fruit delight your eye?
    Did the sampling make you wise?
Hungry Helpmeet, did you gorge and are you sated?
    Was serpent nectar inebriating?
Flesh of flesh and bone of bone, are you now
    Ashamed and naked?
Stitch your fig leaves, worldly Seamstress.
    Do you not find knowledge overrated?

Snakebite

The slitherer that yesterday nipped my toe
took advantage of my naïve belief that it was
safe to traverse from driveway to doorway.
All ten toes—nails cherry painted—were fully
exposed in summer sandals. And I gave no heed
to serpent surveillance. Steps from the car my
ankles were wrapped in coils like those that
clasped Laocoön. The wriggling invader easily
won the bout, offered no signal of remorse,
ate no dust as recompense for his victory.
Thus requited, the narrow fellow glided
among blades and stalks of iris.

In My Garden

    the painted ladies
rise dive flutter and curtsy
    deserve a poem

    september gardens
lure ladies by sight and scent
    they come by thousands

    beneath midday sun
marigolds chives and dahlias—
    butterfly repast

    they dance on air waves
dip swirl glide flit and dazzle
    painted lady waltz

Looking Back

Her tragedy merits only one verse, that
nostalgic female from Sodom. One is enough
to inscribe her metamorphosis upon turning
to view her native city engulfed in brimstone,
fear, regret and flames. She envisions the
graves of her parents, the herb garden of her
dooryard, the underfed cat that often paid a
call, the jolly neighbor with whom she shared
recipes and woman talk.

Luckily for her, she never learned that Lot too
lingered, that in Sodom he offered her daughters
for rape and at Zoar committed incest with them.
Smoke and fire rolled over the cities of the plain,
where Lot's wife was robbed of friendships, relics,
children, future. And her name.

Ravenous

To a child expecting to find her grandmother sunk into
the featherbed, patchwork up to her wattled neck,
it proved quite a shock. The occupier's eyes leered.
He exposed an outsize, black-tipped muzzle, incisors
like stalactites. Wore a familiar nightcap with twitching
lumps atop each side of the head. Very unlike Granny's
dainty ears that resemble matching seashells glued flat
and precise beneath her salt-and-pepper strands.

Awkwardly folded to fit an old lady's single bed, the
stranger spoke comfort in placating tone, the nuance
lascivious, although the child could not label a fear
that weakened her legs, tingled her spine as if an icy
wand traced its length. Perhaps the wolf in granny
clothing signifies desire. But no, this monster devoured
a grandmother. And no virile creature with healthy
self-regard seduces such a bony, stringy dish.

The child cannot know that the intruder—gray-stippled
and amber-eyed—will return. She will be a young woman
spread-eagled with feet in stirrups to accommodate
a birth. Or a matron of middle age, her body invaded
by omnivorous blight. Or a crinkled lady of Granny's
vintage, lying solitary in a narrow bed in a nursing
home. He will slip beneath blanket and sheet, fold her
to his chest, speak her name in his velvety baritone.

Prelude

For Aurore and Mia

George Sand seduced Chopin.
Stooped headlong from Nohant,
a regal raptor clasping easy prey.
The lovers wintered on Majorca,
island of emerald-studded cliffs,
    lapis lazuli sea.

In starlit night, almond-scented, he
embraced as muse an Amazon.
In refracted glow of Apollonian fire, she
did not foresee his gaze avert from
  her face—aging, plain—to alight on
    her daughter, Solange.

Suppliant

Restore Persephone. Too brief is the time
From seedling to harvest, from fledgling to
Flight, from sunrise to pastel afterglow.
One season is scant with a daughter—
A paltry span to suckle and cosset her,
Favor her with nectar and ambrosia,
Oil her body, admire her grace, braid
Her tresses, admonish her not to
Countenance strangers.

Reaper

Il faut que l'herbe pousse et que les enfants meurent.
  - Victor Hugo, *À Villequier*

The Seine is a scythe that cleaves the heart of Paris,
a luminous serpent slithering among ageless icons—
buttressed, arched, golden washed. Her robe, mermaid
green by daylight, transforms to pewter glow at dusk.
She inspires lovers to clamp padlocks on her bridges,
fling the keys into her stream. Alongside her they stroll,
foregrounded in waves of moonlight.

The Seine is Sequana too, river goddess lovely as Lilith.
From the Underworld she erupted as a Bourgogne spring,
shook loose her tresses, flourished her skirt, sauntered
into Paris. There she felled, sheaved, stole pretty children
to adorn her watery chateau—Victor Hugo's beloved
daughter, the babies of Isadora Duncan, a mystery girl
known to the French as L'Inconnue.

Child-keeping

For Marilynne Robinson

I row across a lake of azure, where wispy algae floats
like green cumulous clouds tumbling through heaven.
On dawn's liquid canvas, dappled sunrise refracts
gemstone sparkle. Ashore, I spike marshmallows on
twigs of withered apple trees, the puffed-white scent
rises, drifts, intoxicates. Children come. Peter's Lost Boys
and Golding's, now peaceful, amiable. The Artful Dodger,
adult chapeau perched upon his shock of ragged hair.
Joan the Maid, her shorn head cocked to hear the Voices
explain her escape from burning at Vieux-Marché.
Anne Frank, down from the Secret Annex, careens
her bicycle on pavement, floating ripples of laughter
in her wake. Two little princes, their capes of velvet
brocade—once smudged by mildewed stone and rusted
iron—now bleached by waves that lap and splash as
they traverse the lake, like Jesus treading Galilee.
Kidnapped Nigerian school girls, maidenheads restored,
the atrocities of Boko Haram erased clean as a classroom
whiteboard. Babies baptized in incense of sarin. Infants
whose lullabies were the hum of death falling from
the bellies of aircraft slicing open an aquamarine sky.

Concord Mothers

At Orchard House, two women work
side-by-side throughout a wintry
afternoon. In flickering lamplight they
mend female garments, label with
Sophia's indelible ink a serviceable
wardrobe for Marmee's daughter
deployed to Washington to nurse
the Union's wounded sons.

Mothers are veterans of farewell.
Four years ago Marmee's Lizzie
drifted from her in scorching waves
of scarlet fever. In that same mournful
year Sophia's older girl floated in and
out of consciousness, her mother
love barely sufficient to impede
death's encroaching tide.

So Louisa Alcott packs books and
board games to entertain lads fallen
at Fredericksburg as the mothers print
her name on each shirtwaist and chemise.
In dark December twilight that smothers
houses, streets, railway, Sophia's boy
escorts Marmee's Louisa to the station
where she will embark.

Ocean Camping

For Frank

aligned
parallel in
down-filled
sleeping bags
we listen
incoming
waves
whisper
in measured
sibilants

backfolded
tentflap as
aperture
to Casco Bay
we spy
as seagulls
graze
crustaceans
beached by
outgoing tide

Framing the Scene

(a letter from the artist May Alcott)

Mary Cassatt's Paris studio is luminous with
tapestries, statuary, arranged items of
vertu, paintings in splendid frames.
Beneath an antique hanging lamp
guests pose in carved chairs
placed on Turkish rugs.

Wearing Impressionistic umber satin,
Miss Cassatt serves French pastries
from a dumbwaiter clad in heavy
embroidered linen, streams
chocolat and fluffy *crème*
into delicate china cups.

The Brontës Sit for a Portrait

Arranged in somber pose,
three slender figures—
portrayed alike as serious,
reserved, austere—form a
most proper trio. The
curate's daughters, in
Puritan black and grey,
hardly more than girls,
wear their chestnut tresses
tamped down, tamed—
if one makes allowance for
escaped loops and tendrils.
Three engaging pairs of
eyes avoid the painter's
gaze, stare into far distance.
A ghostly space for the artist
to paint himself is bleared,
smudged, smeared—as
Branwell Brontë, adored son
of promise, was in deed erased
by sisters who walked invisible.

Photogenic

Vagabonding Amelia, Queen of the Air,
claimed to fear only growing old. On
the brink of middle age she slammed a
Lockheed Electra 10E into the South Pacific.
A foolproof guarantee against cronedom,
gray hair, wrinkles, senility.

Shots of Amelia at ease—
Posed atop an airplane snout like
a homecoming queen on parade.
That familiar, gap-toothed smile.
Goggles strapped to an aviator cap
that half-covers her tousled bob. Holding
a gargantuan bouquet. In leather jacket
and jodhpurs, object of our gaze. Her
epicene bosom wreathed with pearls,
slashed by necktie or glammed in furs.

Shots of Amelia in action—
Striding, waving, climbing aboard.
Mounted astride an autogiro, like
a bronc buster settling for the ride.
She caresses a Lockheed Vega, chats
up the boys of the press, fondles a
propeller, tunes a cockpit radio. Hers
is the Puckish style of a gamine, the
insouciance of an androgyne. Gazing
back, Amelia aced eternal youth.

iconic dress

she mince-stepped to the microphone
shrugged off the white mink wrap
that slid obligingly to the floor
she evoked a collective gasp
throughout the crowd
of party faithful
for her getup of
flesh-tone soufflé gauze
glowed transparent below
the lights of Madison Square
Garden revealing she wore no
underwear but anyone having
seen the *Playboy* pose knew
that Marilyn in the buff was
sublime the clinging gown
(skin and beads she said)
was sparkling dazzling
as Marilyn shimmied
and whispered the
birthday song
in breathy
tones as if
she and Jack
were all alone
no White House
Press Corps and no
public hungry for scandal
no Jacqueline and no children
(the sheath fetched 8.4 million)

Stitchery

Pheasant or quail feather-stitches
and rabbit trapunto intersect the
delicate flystitch of smaller birds
etched into snowdusting on frozen
Smoky River. Winter transforms the
river road into a white-on-white sampler
embroidered by painstaking foot traffic.

Selfhood

An artist lives a double life. – Willa Cather

Young Willela absorbed the essence of untarnished country.
Shaggy grassland endless as Nebraska sky. Disc of moon,
wagon-wheel size, suspended among star sparks and fugitive

cloud shred. Dialects of meadowlark, quail, mourning dove.
In summer a scorching brilliant heat to ripen the corn; in winter
a blast that transforms plowed soil into corrugated sheet iron.

From her close-fitting attic bedroom in frontier Red Cloud, she
birthed her second self as William Cather, affected a cocky boyish
manner and masculine apparel. She fell in love with immigrant

Ántonia, lithe and proud as a young cottonwood, her tangle of
curls tinted the copper of turning smartweed, eyes like sunlight
reflected in brown pools of a shaded Bohemian woodland.

Sophia Andreevna Dreams of Trees

In April cherry-blossom fragrance drifted throughout the
Moscow house. From October's window Countess Tolstoy
spied upon trees as they robed in russet and gold.

In numb January she conjured Yasnaya Polyana, woodland
etched in mist, hoarfrost swaddling young evergreens,
Leo Nikolaevich writing, children skating on the pond.

At their estate silver birches lined the driveway, quaking
narrow-leaved summer cascades in twilight like a gaggle
of slender girls in white satin, whispering secrets.

The Tolstoys had planted endless rows of pears, cherries
plums. Antonovka apples—pungent and crisp—for the
Moscow winter. And a fortress of spruce and oak.

As a bride working amid peasant women, Sophia had plied
apart tangles of oak roots, nestled them in the soil, tutored
saplings upright, nurtured an infant forest.

When the couple quarreled, she threatened to die in the
style of Anna Karenina. Instead she took hatchet and saw,
plunged into the orchard and pruned trees.

In hungry years poor serfs pillaged the woodland for winter fuel, left a myriad of black stumps like rental top hats flung about a haberdashery the morning following a gala.

She buried Tolstoy in Zakaz forest, where he had sought the magic green wand of happiness. Whorled branches of spruce were brought by peasants and heaped upon the grave.

.

Anne's Soliloquy

It was insult and afterthought. Once Will had
consigned his fortune to our daughter, his body
to Holy Trinity churchyard and his scribblings
to the ages, he bequeathed to me only the
second-best bed. Oh yes, along with the fittings.
Now busybodies stifle whispers and titters when
they spy me in the marketplace, avert their gaze
when I enter chapel. The goodwife of a famous
Londoner singled out for the indignity of cast-off
furniture. Thrust upon the mercy of sons-in-law,
the village doctor and village ne'er-do-well. With
not so much as tuppence for stockings and gruel.

I was born Anne Hathaway, heir to misfortune.
An orphan with scant dowry, I took a local youth
into my bed. Unschooled he was in the ways
of amour, but quite imaginative. Grant him that.
Perhaps he once considered me fair or fancied
I could teach him to navigate the shores, coves
and inlets of arousal and ecstasy. Our quiet nuptials
made me an *honest* woman. Grant him also that.
But he soon tired of Stratford, declared all his
world a prison, for his thinking made it so. Like a
baited bear, he swiped at the hounds of tedium,
as to great London he turned ambitious thought.

I little thought Will apt to nuzzle peevish babies at
their teething, assist tiny scholars with numbers and
letters. But when my boy died, his poet-father
sentenced me to grieve alone. Sorrow sat in
Hamnet's place at table, filled out his little doublet,
mimicked his laughter. The magistrate's chair was
vacant. He died possessing a manor worthy of his
fame, even a coat of arms. Yet where is justice
for the woman who gave suck to his children,
placated his old parents, endured his wanderlust?
What for me but abasement, grief, regret—
and the bequest of the second-best bed.

Driving West from Mena, Arkansas

My car crawled along the spine of the
Ouachita Mountains just after green buds
had unfurled on twigs and branches and
smoky blue haze canopied the valleys.
I followed the westward trail of ancestors—
Indians expelled from Alabama and
Confederate rebels who Huck-like
lit out for the Territory. Okies were
tough—cowhands, boomers, roughnecks,
gamblers. (All of them gamblers.)
Near Winding Stair Mountain, I pulled
off the road. I hiked into the woods,
cooled down beside a natural spring
in the ravine where Belle Starr and her
horse-thieving husband were said to
water and conceal their ill-gotten stock.
In southeastern Oklahoma everyone
claims a great-granddad who bought
a horse from Belle Starr or after spring's
deluge carried her in his arms across
a flooded creek. My people too left
outsized stories. An unwilling Choctaw
settler murdered in the Indian Removal.
A great-grandfather shot by a bootlegger
over a swig of illegal brew. Others who
preferred to die with boots on but settled

for burial with their lariat. Rodeoers, laborers, homesteaders, ranchers. (And their women who raised kids as they raised hell.) I wonder if any of them met a notorious woman named Belle.

Obsession

How can she fail to know, Lois Lane,
that the steady journalist Kent is the
heartthrob of her dreamlife? Is she
oblivious to his amble or stride? Hasn't
she been tempted to touch his hair—
glossy, thick, waving, impeccably
groomed? How can she not identify
the quizzical lift of his brow, length
and density of lashes, glints and shards
that compose the color of his eyes?
As he sits at his *Daily Planet* desk,
does she not observe the degree
and angle that he spreads his long
legs, his peculiar flexing of muscles
in back and shoulders, the way he
holds a pencil or his coffee cup?
When his alter ego shows up street
level on Planet Earth, sans necktie and
eyeglasses and decked out in comic
book redandblue, can she not smell
the familiar musk-and-herbal cocktail
of aftershave and shampoo? Hasn't
she studied the breadth of his hand,
taper of fingers, the very shape that
he trims his nails? Didn't she notice

that today his razor mowed over
a chin crevice, leaving a dark row of
micro-stubble in the landscape of his
lower face? Until you have itemized
and memorized each aspect of his being,
Lois Lane, you surely cannot call it love.

A Litany

(from Frida Kahlo's journal)

Diego my father, mother, brother, creator
(in my arms, on my breast, on my brow)
Diego my infant, offspring, surviving son
(baby among bulrushes, love embrace)
Diego my bridegroom, husband, lover
(titan, tormentor, source, obsession)
Diego my alpha omega, without within
(muse, maker, leader, visionary, curse)
Diego my eye and I, Diego my Universe.

Frida Imagines

Woman's amniotic fluid rains from a swollen
womb, ripe with infant fruit. From the Great
Mother's great brown breasts leak iridescent
drops, shining like pearls.

Woman's tears spill from a trussed patient on a
hospital bed, dampen a Tehuana dress. They fall
from eyes of still life coconuts and labia of
sliced mangos, the droplets as seeds.

Woman's blood soaks a mattress, drips beneath
a thorn necklace, trickles petal-shaped from
sutures, sprinkles a fecund jungle floor, dyes
a red flower on a white wedding dress.

Woman flows, spouts, splashes, courses, floods.
Woman suffers, engenders, nourishes, dies, endures.

Woman Wall, 2019

five million women
wrapped in showy
silk saris, colors to
rival a Kerala rainbow,
fuchsia rose lilac pink
tints of flower petals,
costly amber ruby
emerald sapphire,
edible mint plum
melon apricot, gold
bangles, hoop and
dangle earrings,
pendants anklets rings,
vermilion bindi dots
on foreheads;
menstruating mothers
attorneys and techies
athletes and teachers
ample grandmas and
spindling daughters,
five million fists raised
form a 500-kilometer
female barricade
warning Sabarimala
of intent to penetrate
a mortar wall, defile
a holy Hindu temple.

Tables Turned

Napoleon declared Paris too small
for himself and Germaine de Staël,
decreed for her all the world beside,
the capitol for the Emperor. Exiled
from Paris as Dante from Florence,
Madame wrote, *Daily the Emperor
commits more insolence than
monarchs manage in a year.*

After a decade she returned to reign
as *salonnière*. In her aristocracy of wit,
the *bon mot* became the coin of
commerce. In his Inferno Napoleon
heard that all of Paris now was hers.

Penelope's Lament

Reeking of salt and sex, my Odysseus
has returned from the wine-dark sea.
His beard grizzled, visage browned
by sun and travel, furrowed by the
scheming that saved him at Ilium
and in tussles with a vengeful deity.
His pocket stuffed with seashells
and Trojan coins for Telemachus;
his mouth stuffed with exploits,
adventures, boasts, excuses. Truth
be told, Ithaca is a hard place. We
ply the Ionian Sea to fill our bowls,
graze sure-footed goats on rock
terrain, assault earth, air and water
for that which we wear and eat.
I too have become hard.
I am a part of all that I have met—
all that came to Ithaca to meet me.
Bards will recount them every one.
Old Laertes' fine-wrought shroud.
Brawling suitors devouring our board.
Solitary grief in the olive-tree bed.
Impudence of our grownup son.

Love Letter

(a found poem)

June 17, 1944

Sweetheart Husband,
Night being the loneliest time, I reflect how brief
has been our life as newly marrieds. Did the Navy
cut off your lovely curls first thing? And could you
have a picture taken in your sailor blues? Then
I might see your smile and think how proud I am
to have my sailor training for whatever you will
be assigned, although I know you could never
say just what. Was your birthday cake all broken
up when it arrived? Today I got your letter saying
you have plenty of time to waste so please be
careful. I imagine San Diego a dangerous place—
sailors cutting loose, guzzling in bars, swaggering
on the streets, looking for a fight. I worry about
the twenty bottles of beer you say the Navy gives
you every month. And I didn't laugh when you
wrote that you don't get drunk oftener than
you did before you were drafted. The kid gloves
I ordered finally came. And I bought a pale blue
slacks suit that must be taken in an inch about the
waist for when you get furlough. Until then I daily
X off a number on my calendar. Next Wednesday
the hired hands will begin baling hay on Fred's

place, if Dad's wired-up baler holds out another
week. For 25 cents per bale they produce, I'll
cook dinner and supper to serve the haying crew.
I wouldn't be out there on the meadow with all
those boys except that my brothers are among
them. I know you won't think bad of me if I go
into the field to feed the hands, for I have earned
not one penny since you left. Go ahead and buy
yourself a new suit if you want. And the hat too.
But you were just joking about the pistol, weren't
you? The kerosene in the lamp is burning low,
so I say good-bye and promise to dream your face
tonight and every night until you come home to
Your loving wife

Only Mother milked the cow

because, she said, with only the one milker,
if children tried, Bossie might go dry. Mother
would offer the wary cow a handful of cattle
nuggets, speak her name, stroke her neck, edge
cowlength to the rear.

She chose the right side, settled on a downturned
pail near teats and hindquarters, turned face left,
leaned in—woman cheek to bovine loin. As she
murmured, her rhythmic fingers squeezed, her
brunette beauty a cameo on Jersey background
colored like ripe wheat.

Mother had a penchant for adopting barnyard runts
rejected by herd or flock: she raised a chick in a
cardboard box, laid a piglet to rest, gentled a lame
skunk that arrived at dusk to nibble from her spoon.
Near the last she nested between an ancient Poodle
and a frowzy Pekingese.

I suspect that Mother lied about the cow going dry,
that she hoarded moments with Bossie, away from
callow offspring, whose tether to livestock and land
stretched gossamer fine as spider webs crisscrossing
the open corral gate.

Temperance Warrior

With bricks and hatchets Carry and the Smashers
    blasted Kansas saloons like tornadic winds
        that whack and splinter, wallop
            and fracture.

Often Carry A. Nation crusaded alone, for only she
    heard God's charge to demolish dens
        of iniquity in Medicine Lodge
            and Kiowa.

Six feet tall and calm as a grenadier, she lobbed
    a haymaker that unmanned purveyors
        and clients who *tarried*
            at the wine.

She chose a Wichita hotel for its swanky nightclub,
    not only bludgeoned fittings and utensils but
        slashed the naked lady painting
            above the bar.

In Topeka's Senate saloon she clobbered slot machines,
    cash register, beer tubing, a barkeep's
        composure, the prestige of
            senatorial imbibers.

Carry would tip over a keg of ale and cleave it with her
weapon, releasing spume and splash grand as
Old Faithful. (She sold replica hatchets
to go her bail.)

For Peace, Bread and Roses

It took five jolts to stall her obdurate heart.
Upon the fifth, smoke roiled from her head
as a rabbi intoned the 23rd Psalm. Given her
icy staredown of prosecutor and Reaper, the
state could not expect a ladylike demise. She
wept no womanly tears, made no mother's
plea. (The jury found her guilty of having no
maternal streak.) Literati reviled the verdict, a
Pope entreated clemency, Presidential pardon
was begged in letters to Mamie and Ike.

Ethel Rosenberg spoke no final words.

I wonder if she knew Yiddish. Took her boys
to the museum on Sunday afternoons. Read
the existentialists. Had she to do it over,
would she embrace martyrdom?
For what ephemeral peace?
Bread for whose bellies?
What blighted roses?

Early Redbud

Like a floating insect
embalmed in amber,
each magenta embryo
on the redbud tree is
encased in a perfect globe
of ice—kernel of garnet
glinting inside crystal—
until the tiny sarcophagi
melt in midday sun and
a million stillborn corpses
flutter to their grave.

Just Ourselves and Immortality

From Oklahoma hill country comes word of the
winnowing of my peers. Maureen, the Pentecostal girl,
who in study hall announced that her palms glittered
with holy oil. The pilot Victor, whose Icarus boyhood
plummeted into adulthood behind bars, sentenced
for flying as cargo the illicit ambrosia of Colombia.
Jimmy's Sarah, who filched his pistol and shot herself as
antidote to the cancer that defiled her. Petite Wanda Jo,
retreating, fading into misty dementia. My first molester
too has shuffled off his mortal coil, although I am not
told the means of his exit. I recall them dribbling
basketballs, dragging Main, sneaking a smoke behind
the gym, flirting at Dairy Dream. Lucky, myopic youth,
unable to fathom another self—shambling halt, palsied,
harmless into that good night.

Modern Pastoral

Saturday afternoons, autumn and spring,
we filled a hamper with snacks and cokes
and fled campus in your '55 Chevrolet.
You left-handedly herded the Chevy
onto a gravel country road, your right hand
embracing my shoulder like an emphatic
parenthesis close. We hummed to Sam Cooke
crooning "You-ou-ou send me," drove past
farms nested in landscaped groves, grazing
cattle, a NO TRESSPASSING sign dangling
from a post oak beside the road. You inched the
Chevy into a shallow ditch beside somebody's
wood or crop or meadow. With hamper and
folded blanket, we slipped between strung lines
of somebody's barbed wire. You unfurled the
faded blanket and spread it with panache, like
Sir Walter flourishing a cape to spare the slippers
of his queen. We nested on our pirated square
of somebody's landscape. Beside his stream,
beneath his foliage canopy, or lounging on his
sun-speckled hillside, we opened our hamper,
popped cola tabs, swallowed cold swigs. Those
were delicious afternoons, punctuated by
bob-bob-white whistles, fanned by breezes that
shivered leaves and riffled the wild-grass
meadow. But I expected Somebody—shotgun
balanced on strong, broad shoulder—to appear
around a bend of his stream or rise above
undulations of his violated acres.

Notes:

In "Snakebite," a phrase describing the snake is appropriated from Emily Dickinson's poem "A narrow Fellow in the Grass."

Several images in "Selfhood" are adapted from Willa Cather's fiction, especially from *My Àntonia*.

"Anne's Soliloquy" slightly misquotes Shakespeare's Hamlet, who complains that all the world's a prison. The comment on the Shakespeares' dead son is based upon that of a grieving mother in *King John*.

In "Penelope's Lament," I borrow a familiar line from "Ulysses," by Alfred, Lord Tennyson.

"Just Ourselves and Immortality" takes its title from Dickinson's "Because I could not stop for Death." The phrase "shuffled off [this] mortal coil" is from *Hamlet*, and the final line alludes to "Do Not Go Gentle into that Good Night," by Dylan Thomas.

"Tender but tough." That's how one poet characterized Linda M. Lewis's poems of love and spite, loss and triumph. Linda gratefully accepts the appraisal. A professor emerita of Bethany College in Lindsborg, Kansas, she has been an activist, critic, educator, editor, wife, mother, and grandparent. She is the author of numerous critical essays and four books: *The Promethean Politics of Milton, Blake, and Shelley*; *Elizabeth Barrett Browning's Spiritual Progress*; *Germaine de Staël, George Sand, and the Victorian Woman Artist*; and *Dickens, His Parables, and His Reader*. This is her first volume of verse.

This project was made possible, in part, by generous support from the Osage Arts Community.

Osage Arts Community provides temporary time, space and support for the creation of new artistic works in a retreat format, serving creative people of all kinds — visual artists, composers, poets, fiction and nonfiction writers. Located on a 152-acre farm in an isolated rural mountainside setting in Central Missouri and bordered by ¾ of a mile of the Gasconade River, OAC provides residencies to those working alone, as well as welcoming collaborative teams, offering living space and workspace in a country environment to emerging and mid-career artists. For more information, visit us at www.osageac.org

www.ingramcontent.com/pod-product-compliance
Lightning Source LLC
Chambersburg PA
CBHW030133100526
44591CB00009B/629